A Celebration of the Civil Rights Movement ™

THE EMANCIPATION PROCLAMATION AND THE END OF SLAVERY IN AMERICA

Diane Bailey

ROSEN
PUBLISHING®

New York

Published in 2015 by The Rosen Publishing Group, Inc.
29 East 21st Street, New York, NY 10010

Copyright © 2015 by The Rosen Publishing Group, Inc.

First Edition

Library of Congress Cataloging-in-Publication Data

Bailey, Diane.
The Emancipation Proclamation and the end of slavery in America/by Diane Bailey, first edition.
    p. cm. – (A celebration of the civil rights movement)
Includes bibliographical references and index.
ISBN 978-1-4777-7749-7 (library binding)
1. Lincoln, Abraham, 1809–1865 – Juvenile literature. 2. United States. President (1861–1865 : Lincoln). Emancipation Proclamation – Juvenile literature. 3. Slaves – Emancipation – United States – Juvenile literature. 4. United States – Politics and government – 1861–1865 – Juvenile literature. I. Bailey, Diane, 1966–. II. Title.
E453.B38 2015
973.7–d23

Manufactured in the United States of America

Cover caption: A large part of the U.S. economy, slaves were bought and sold at markets during the first half of the 1800s. President Abraham Lincoln would forever change that through his actions during the Civil War.

CONTENTS

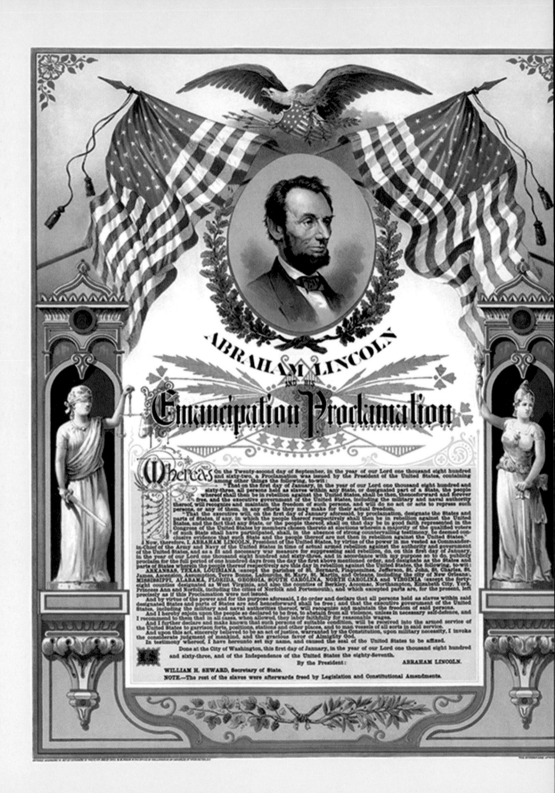

M ore than a thousand Republican delegates crowded into the statehouse in Springfield, Illinois, on June 16, 1858. They had nominated Abraham Lincoln to be their candidate for the upcoming Senate election, and now, on that late spring evening, they waited for him to speak.

Lincoln went on to deliver a stirring speech, one in which he predicted that the United States would face huge problems with slavery. "A house divided against itself cannot stand," Lincoln said. "I believe this government cannot endure, permanently half *slave* and half *free*. I do not expect the Union to be *dissolved*—I do not expect the house to *fall*—but I do expect it will cease to be divided. It will become *all* one thing or *all* the other."

The campaign had barely begun, but Lincoln's speech helped position him as an antislavery candidate—and it

This depiction of the Emancipation Proclamation suggests the idea of freedom and justice, with the text of the document topped off by Abraham Lincoln's picture and the American flag.

probably caused him to lose the Senate election. Yet Lincoln's words would come true. Three years later, the Civil War would begin, in large part because of slavery. Lincoln, who had moved up through the political ranks and was now president of the country, was forced to deal with the issue head-on. For more than a year, Lincoln tried to get the states to abolish slavery voluntarily. When that didn't work, he indicated he would do it himself by issuing the Emancipation Proclamation. If he did so, it would be a monumental act—and there was a substantial chance it would backfire, leaving the country more entrenched in slavery than ever. Would he follow through?

On the morning of New Year's Day in 1863, the nation anxiously awaited to see what the president would do. It appeared that not even his wife, Mary Todd Lincoln, knew his final decision. She asked him at breakfast. Lincoln glanced upward, as if looking to the heavens. Perhaps he had made a promise to God because he replied, "I am a man under orders; I cannot do otherwise."

Still, it was a nervous, nail-biting kind of morning. The Proclamation returned from the printer at about 10:45 AM, but when he was proofreading the document, Lincoln noticed a mistake. The copyist had incorrectly written a phrase. At the end, instead of reading, "In *witness* whereof I have hereunto set my *hand*," the document said, "In *testimony* whereof I have hereunto set my *name*." It seemed like a small difference, but it was important. Lincoln sent it back.

As he waited for the corrected version, he had a party to attend. In keeping with tradition, Lincoln hosted a White

House get-together to celebrate the New Year. For hours, Lincoln conversed with his guests, shaking hands the whole time. By mid-afternoon the event had ended, and Lincoln headed back to his office to sign the final Proclamation. As his advisers looked on, Lincoln picked up his pen—and then set it down again. Later, Lincoln would recall that his hands were shaking. Was it a sign? Was he wrong? For a year and a half, Lincoln had tried to avoid this moment. But there was no more waiting.

Again, he took up his pen.

Chapter 1

A WAR-TORN COUNTRY

Worry lines creased the president's face as the clack-clack-clack of the telegraph brought its news. As the Civil War raged on, weeks turning into months, Lincoln spent hours in the White House telegraph office, anxiously awaiting reports from the field. The Union armies were scattered throughout the eastern portion of the country, struggling to put down the Confederate troops. Sometimes, the latest news brought a small sigh of relief. Other times, the staccato clicking of the machine brought dismay, as the Confederacy gained ground.

As the rift between the North and the South widened, Lincoln had just one goal: preserve the Union. Somehow, some way, he wanted to bring the country through the greatest crisis it had ever seen. But how?

SLAVERY VS. STATES' RIGHTS

For over 150 years, historians have debated this question: What caused the Civil War? Some people say it was slavery. Others say it was about allowing states to exercise their constitutional rights. In fact, it is a bit of both. Moral objections to slavery were gaining ground in the United States by the

African American slaves pick cotton on a plantation in this drawing created in about 1800. This backbreaking work was crucial to the economy of the Southern states.

middle of the nineteenth century. At the same time, however, the country's economy depended on slave labor, especially in the South. The Southern economy was based on large-scale agriculture. Farmers grew cotton, tobacco, and other crops on huge plantations. There was a lot of work to do, and the system relied on slave labor. Slaves were considered to be property. They were bought and sold, just like land or machines. They had virtually no rights. However, there was a law that counted each slave as three-fifths of a person. That gave the Southern states more power in Congress.

THE PECULIAR INSTITUTION

Southerners often referred to slavery as "our peculiar institution." In this context, the word "peculiar" did not mean odd, but rather unique to a particular society or region. The phrase was in wide use during Civil War times because the word "slavery" was considered unacceptable. In fact, although the Constitution permitted slavery, nowhere in that document is the word actually mentioned.

People who favored social change wanted to do away with slavery. Southern leaders believed this would cripple their economy. They objected, arguing that slavery was legal (which was true), and that the federal government had no right to interfere with something that was constitutionally approved. States' rights, they said, were the business of the states, not the federal government.

Even those who opposed slavery did not always do so on moral grounds. Many Northerners supported abolition precisely for the same reason the South opposed it—it gave the Southern states an economic advantage.

THE RISE OF THE REPUBLICANS

Put the economic and ethical issues around slavery together, and it became a thorny political issue, too. By the middle of the 1800s, tensions had been rising for years, and in 1854, the Republican Party was founded on an antislavery platform.

Still considered one of America's greatest presidents, Abraham Lincoln was elected in 1860, just as the country was beginning the long, painful era of the Civil War.

Throughout the second half of the 1850s, Lincoln became a leading Republican. In February 1860, he gave a speech at Cooper Union in New York City. In this address, he supported a national policy of not allowing slavery to spread into the federal territories. At the time, that included most of the West (excluding California and Oregon, which were already states). Unlike states, the territories were under direct federal control. Lincoln's antislavery position helped him get the 1860 presidential nomination from the Republican Party.

Still, Lincoln understood that slavery was constitutional, and legal, in the Southern states. When he was running for president, he assured these states that he had no "inclination" to interfere with slavery. Some have interpreted this to mean that he approved of slavery—or at best didn't care. Others argue that it had a more literal meaning. He wasn't "inclined" to meddle only because he couldn't—it was the law of the land.

The results from the presidential election of 1860 already showed a country in turmoil. Lincoln won, but not by a majority. Four candidates were on the ballot that year. Lincoln carried only a plurality of the vote—more than any other single candidate, but not more than 50 percent of the total. A map shows that Lincoln's support was almost entirely in the North, while the South solidly voted for one of his opponents, John Breckenridge.

Plenty of people wanted a different president, so when Lincoln won, becoming the nation's first Republican president, the South was outraged. They would not stand for a president who threatened their way of life. Tensions were already high, and Lincoln's election was the final straw. Seven weeks after the election, on December 20, 1860, South

THE HAITIAN REVOLUTION

Count Mirabeau, a French writer living in the late eighteenth century, had some words of warning for the white people who lived in the French territory of Saint-Domingue (now the Central American country of Haiti). They enslaved thousands of blacks, and the threat of a slave rebellion was constant. Mirabeau wrote that whites "slept at the foot of Vesuvius," a reference to the volcano that erupted and destroyed the city of Pompeii in ancient times. In the summer of 1791, Mirabeau's words came true. The slaves revolted, and a violent struggle ensued that lasted for months. By the end of it, blacks had overthrown their white masters. Slavery was formally abolished in 1794, and the nation of Haiti was founded a decade later. As the Civil War approached, American slaveholders feared their slaves might successfully revolt, too.

Count Mirabeau's dire predictions came true after slaves in Saint-Domingue revolted against their French masters, who had refused to give them the rights that France guaranteed them.

Carolina became the first state to secede from the Union.

Four months later, when the Civil War officially began, Mississippi, Florida, Alabama, Georgia, Louisiana, and Texas had also seceded. Within two more months, four additional states—Virginia, Arkansas, North Carolina, and Tennessee—would join the Confederacy. The Union was comprised of 20 "free" states in the North, which did not allow slavery, as well as four "border" states—Kentucky, Missouri, Maryland, and Delaware—that allowed slavery but nonetheless remained loyal to the Union. The country was firmly divided. Ironically, the man whose election had triggered the Civil War would become the man charged with trying to end it.

SQUEEZING THE SOUTH

The question was how to do so. Many "radical Republicans" wanted slavery abolished. They were itching for the president to declare a new policy that made slavery illegal nationwide. Not only did they think it was morally the

Only weeks after Lincoln was elected president, South Carolina seceded from the Union. Supporters of states' rights hoisted a flag to assert their independence from the country.

right thing to do, they also believed it would also help the Union win the war.

In the early months of the Civil War, slavery gave the Southern states a military advantage. With thousands of slaves performing free labor, white Southerners were able to leave their plantations and join the Confederate Army. Some even put their slaves to work directly on the war cause, having them help build forts or gather supplies for soldiers. Slavery had been a cause of the Civil War, and now it was helping to sustain it.

Another factor to consider was the international community. Although the Civil War was being waged exclusively on American soil, Europe took a keen interest in its progress. The Southern states were major producers of cotton, much of which was exported to Europe. As the war progressed, Union forces disrupted the transportation and supply channels on which the South depended. As a result, less cotton made it to Europe, and that threatened its economy.

Europe, especially Britain, was also affected by U.S. "free trade" policies. The Northern economy favored imposing high tariffs on products imported from Britain. The South supported less restricted trade, which would help the British economy. A win for the South, then, could help Britain. As the war progressed, there were indications that Britain might offer military aid to the South. By the spring and summer of 1862, the North was already losing. If the Confederacy got more help, it could be disastrous for the Union.

Again, radical Republicans pointed out that emancipation would discourage Europe from entering the war. Britain and France had already outlawed slavery. If the United States—the

North—did so as well, those nations would be hard-pressed to support the pro-slavery Confederacy over the antislavery Union.

The president, however, did not immediately follow the abolitionists' advice. As commander-in-chief, he had to think about the big picture. He had to consider all the consequences of emancipation: moral and military, economic and social, legal and political. Like anyone, Lincoln had certain beliefs about what was right and wrong. He once said, "I am naturally antislavery. If slavery is not wrong, nothing is wrong." As he had predicted in his famous "House Divided" speech, slavery was tearing the country apart. But as president, his job was to uphold the law of the land—and that included slavery. What he hoped to do was find a way around this seemingly impossible dilemma.

Chapter 2

NO EASY ANSWERS

"I hope to have God on my side, but I must have Kentucky." Those words are sometimes attributed to Lincoln. He probably never actually said them, but he likely thought something along those lines. As he searched for a way to end the war, Lincoln believed the answer lay in the power of the border states.

A BORDER BUYOUT

At the outbreak of the Civil War, the border states had remained loyal to the Union side. However, they were also slave states. If slavery was abolished, as many Northerners were urging Lincoln to do, the economies of the border states could suffer. They might jump to the Confederate cause. If that happened, the Union would likely lose the war and slavery would be reinstated—if indeed it had ever left. Lincoln had an idea. Maybe he could ease the financial burden on the border states, at the same time showing the South that slavery could end without more bloodshed.

THE COST OF FREEDOM

Some people objected that Lincoln's plan for compensated emancipation would bankrupt the government. Lincoln responded by pointing out that the Union spent some $2,000,000 for each day of fighting. In contrast, he was suggesting purchasing roughly 450,000 slaves, in all the border states and the District of Columbia, at an average of $400 apiece. That would cost less than fighting the war for three months. However, the price Lincoln was offering came in below the market value, where slaves could bring $1,500 each. And, of course, the payment only covered the slaves themselves, not all the turmoil that would come as an entire social system was dismantled.

Lincoln believed that emancipation needed the support of the people and should be a voluntary decision. To make the idea of emancipation attractive to the border states, he proposed that they free their slaves gradually and that the federal government pay them for the loss of their property.

For months, Lincoln urged leaders from the border states to accept his buyout plan. He hoped that if the Southern states saw that slavery was on its way out, it would convince them to back down and rejoin the Union. Then, the institution of slavery would gradually be phased out. A buyout move would also take advantage of economics. With fewer slaveholding states, the demand for slaves would decrease. That would drive down their price, since fewer people would be competing to buy them. Thus, it made sense for slave owners to voluntarily free their slaves and be compensated early in the process, while the price was still relatively high.

Lincoln's plan could be considered a bribe. However, it was a perfectly legal one, and staying within the law was exactly Lincoln's goal. Certainly, purchasing slaves would cost the government money. It wasn't as morally superior as simply freeing them for ethical considerations alone. But it would get the job done, and the plan avoided any legal challenges about seizing property or violating the states' rights. Despite Lincoln's attempts to persuade them, however, the slaveholding states firmly, and repeatedly, rejected the idea of gradual emancipation.

MILITARY MANEUVERS

While state lawmakers were reluctant to accept change, the situation was much different on the field of battle. Slavery was providing manpower to the Southern cause. If the South could be cut off from using its slave labor, it would weaken its forces considerably. In other words, emancipation could shorten the war. Lincoln's military commanders saw this—and some decided to make it work in their favor.

In May 1861, Union major general Benjamin Butler was in command at Fort

Monroe in Virginia when three escaped slaves showed up, seeking protection. The Fugitive Slave Act of 1850 stated that runaway slaves had to be returned to their masters. However, Butler decided other factors were at work. For one thing, the

The Union base of Fort Monroe in Virginia, shown here in an 1860 drawing, became a hot spot after General Benjamin Butler harbored runaway slaves, setting the stage for similar future actions.

slaves had been engaged in helping their masters with the Confederate cause. Moreover, they were not considered citizens, but merely "property." Butler reasoned that this gave him the right to seize the slaves as contraband—property taken from enemy forces.

On August 30, 1861, Union general John Frémont took things another step when he declared martial law in Missouri, one of the border states. He ordered that all slave owners who were in rebellion against the Union had to free their slaves. Frémont was overstepping his bounds, though. He had made a political decision, not a military one. The order clearly infringed on the rights of Missouri citizens. Another problem was how these slaves would be handled after the war. The military could not permanently keep seized assets. That meant that, in theory, the slaves could be returned to their owners after the war.

Lincoln feared rash decisions such as Frémont's could push the border states into the Confederacy. He asked Frémont to back down, but the general refused. Left with no other choice, Lincoln overruled him and rescinded the order.

Many abolitionists were frustrated that Lincoln did not back up Frémont, but Lincoln urged them to be patient. He wasn't ignoring the problem; he was considering it. In a letter to a pro-abolitionist, Rev. Charles Edwards Lester, Lincoln wrote, "I think...you would upset our applecart if you had your way. We'll fetch 'em; just give us a little time. We didn't go into the war to put down slavery, but to put the flag back, and to act differently at this moment would, I have no doubt, not only weaken our cause but smack of bad faith; for I never should have had votes enough to send me here if the people had supposed I should try to use my power to upset slavery.

Union General John Frémont declared martial law in Missouri and attempted to free slaves there, but Lincoln overturned the order, concerned that in the long run it would hurt the Union cause.

Why, the first thing you'd see, would be a mutiny in the army. No, we must wait until every other means has been exhausted. This thunderbolt will keep."

Lincoln was upholding the law—but he was also working on that "big picture." He hadn't said "never"; he had said "wait." When the time was right, he had his thunderbolt.

THE CONFISCATION ACTS

Congress was also moving against the South. After General Butler seized the fugitive slaves, the nation's legislators passed laws to legalize such actions. In August 1861, they passed the First Confiscation Act. This law allowed the Union military to confiscate slaves whom the Confederates were using to support military actions against the Union. A year later, in 1862, Congress passed the Second Confiscation Act. This freed any slaves who belonged to a person in rebellion against the Union, whether or not the slave was directly helping the Confederate cause.

Lincoln questioned the legality of the Confiscation Acts, but Congress justified them by arguing they were aimed at individual people in rebellion, not the states themselves. There was another problem, though. Lincoln was treating the war as a domestic rebellion—meaning that one part of the country was in rebellion against the other, but that the conflict was not between two different countries. In other words, he refused to recognize the Confederacy as its own nation. This meant that Confederates were still U.S. citizens, and taking their property without payment was unconstitutional. In addition, freeing slaves was easier in theory than it

DEFINING LIBERTY

What, exactly, was "liberty"? As the country took sides, Lincoln used a story to illustrate the problem. If a shepherd drove a wolf away from his flock of sheep, the sheep would appreciate him protecting their freedom. However, the wolf would object that the shepherd had interfered with his ability to hunt the sheep. Obviously, the sheep and the wolf did not agree on the definition of "freedom." In this parable, the sheep represented slaves, the wolf represented the slave owner, and the shepherd was Lincoln himself. Lincoln chose to pursue a course of "positive liberty," meaning he wanted to protect the right of individuals—in this case, blacks—to lead their own lives.

was in practice. Southern slaveholders weren't going to simply let them go, and most slaves did not have the resources to escape. Thus, unless the Union Army was physically present to free them, they remained where they were.

In May of 1862, another Union general, David Hunter, declared the slaves in his region (South Carolina, Georgia, and Florida) to be free—even if their owners were not actively fighting the Union. Some criticized Hunter and said he was misusing his authority. Others supported his decision and said it was vital to the military cause. Carl Schurz, one of Lincoln's associates, advised Lincoln that Hunter's action was just a preview of what had to happen eventually. He advised Lincoln to let the order stand. If the president supported it, Schurz reasoned, so would the people.

Engraved by J. C. Buttre

MAJ. GEN. DAVID HUNTER.

Union General David Hunter was in charge of the war effort in several Southern states. In 1862, he declared slaves in his region free, but as Lincoln had done before, he revoked the order.

Ten days after Hunter's proclamation, however, Lincoln revoked it. In his response, he hinted at what was to come. He did not say Hunter was wrong, exactly. Instead, he wrote that if freeing slaves should become necessary, he would do it himself. He also used the statement to once again urge the border states to voluntarily emancipate their slaves, pointing out that they should not "be blind to the signs of the times." Again, the answer was no. With time, the states might come to accept Lincoln's offer. But by the middle of 1862, Lincoln was out of time. The Union was floundering, and Europe was on the brink of offering aid to the Confederacy. Lincoln realized that he needed to flip-flop his strategy. He could not use the border states as a way to lead the Confederacy back into the Union. Instead, he needed to go straight to the South itself. It was time to get tough.

Chapter 3

BIDING HIS TIME

It wasn't quite business as usual on April 16, 1862. That day, Lincoln signed a bill that ended slavery in the District of Columbia, which was under federal jurisdiction. The new law freed only about three thousand slaves, but it sent a message about what was coming. Although few people knew about it yet, Lincoln had decided to issue the Emancipation Proclamation, which would affect far more slaves—and he was already hard at work writing it.

A FIRST DRAFT

Before the days of air-conditioning and automatic icemakers, summer in the White House was hot, humid, and stuffy. Soldiers' Home, a residence for disabled veterans located a few miles north of the White House, was quieter and more peaceful than the White House. A gentle breeze kept things cooler. In June 1862, the Lincoln family moved to a cottage on the grounds.

THE WRITE PLACE

No one knows exactly where Lincoln actually wrote the Emancipation Proclamation, since he kept it a close secret. Historical paintings show him at work in his study. In other accounts, he wrote it at the Soldiers' Home, in the War Department telegraph office, or on a steamship as he was coming home from a visit to soldiers stationed in Virginia. Perhaps it was some combination of those—or somewhere else entirely. One witness from the telegraph office remembered the words did not seem to come easily: "He would look out of the window for a while, and then put his pen to paper, but did not write much at once."

Artist David Gilmour Blythe imagined Lincoln as he was writing the Proclamation. Blythe envisioned Lincoln in his pajamas, with the Bible and the Constitution close at hand.

It offered a haven from the frenzy of the White House, yet there were still constant reminders of the war. To get to the cottage, Lincoln had to pass by "contraband camps" populated with slaves who had escaped to safety in the Union. Occasionally, as he commuted back and forth to the White House, the president would stop to speak with them. Only Lincoln knew how this sight affected him, but in the year since the Civil War had begun, the president was beginning to back away from his position that the federal government should not interfere with slavery.

During the spring and summer of 1862, Lincoln wrote a draft of the Emancipation Proclamation. If it was put into

CHANNELING GEORGE WASHINGTON?

Lincoln had deep respect for George Washington and often spoke about the country's first president. Washington was born on February 22, and key dates related to the Emancipation Proclamation also fell on the 22nd of the month. Lincoln first announced it to his cabinet on July 22, answered a newspaper editorial on August 22, and released the preliminary Proclamation on September 22. Historians have wondered whether this was a coincidence, or whether Lincoln was "playing the numbers" a bit!

force, it would free the slaves in the Southern states. This huge shift in policy was unprecedented—but then again, so was the war itself.

On July 22, Lincoln showed the document to some of his advisers. They were so surprised that they did not even know how to react. After all, Lincoln had repeatedly said that the federal government would not interfere with slavery. However, Lincoln had made his decision. When he read the Proclamation to them, he did not want advice about its basic purpose or content, only about whether he had worded it well.

BUILDING A CASE

Lincoln's most immediate challenge was how to keep things legal. Slavery was constitutional, so Lincoln needed a workaround to justify emancipation. *The War Powers of the President,* a book written in early 1862 by William Whiting, a lawyer for the War Department, gave Lincoln the foundation he needed. Whiting determined that abolishing slavery could be considered constitutional if it was not a *goal* of the war, but rather a *method* for ending it. Thus, Lincoln conceived of the Proclamation not as a law, but as a military order. It could be instituted during a time of war. That made it temporary—but it was a start.

Another problem was gaining political support. Obviously, emancipation was not going to be popular with Southern slaveholders. A more delicate issue was Lincoln's support among Northerners. Many of them opposed slavery, but that was not exactly the same as saying they supported emancipation.

Some people—the "radical Republicans"—supported abolition on purely ethical grounds. However, many people were
more conservative. A prime reason many Northerners favored
abolition was to even up the economic balance between the
North and the South. Few people, even in the North, actually
believed that African Americans should be considered abso-
lutely equal to whites.

A large segment of Northerners feared that if the slaves were
freed, they would migrate to Northern cities. They would take
jobs and houses that had formerly been reserved for whites.
Racial tensions would soar. Meanwhile, some Southerners
feared that slaves, who were often perceived as hostile savages,
would rise up in violence against their former owners.

Lincoln offered a solution to this dilemma: colonization.
He proposed that the freed slaves could leave the United
States and live elsewhere—perhaps in Africa or Haiti. This
idea had huge drawbacks. It would be expensive and difficult
to organize. In addition, many blacks were not interested
in leaving their home country. Frederick Douglass was one
of the few influential black leaders of the 1860s. He wrote
a newspaper article about the issue early in 1862. Its title
reflected the question on the minds of many: "What Shall
Be Done with the Slaves If Emancipated?" Douglass offered
a biting response: "Our [African Americans'] answer is, do
nothing with them; mind your business, and let them mind
theirs. Your doing with them is their greatest misfortune.
They have been undone by your doings, and all they now
ask, and really have need of at your hands, is just to let them
alone." Nonetheless, in the first draft of the Proclamation,
Lincoln advocated colonization.

Frederick Douglass was one of only a handful of influential African Americans in the mid-1800s. Douglass supported emancipation, but at times he and Lincoln differed on how to best accomplish it.

GETTING THE PEOPLE READY

Lincoln knew the Proclamation would make some people happy—namely, the radical Republicans who opposed slavery and were eager for it to be abolished. But it would make plenty of people unhappy. Crusades need leaders, but they need followers as well. Lincoln knew that if he didn't have support, his plan would ultimately fail.

Timing was critical. Lincoln later recalled that if he had issued the Proclamation any earlier, or any later, it wouldn't have worked. Throughout July and August, only a few people knew about the Proclamation. It had not yet been publicly issued. During this time, Lincoln took several steps to ready the public for what was to come.

On August 14, Lincoln met with a group of black leaders at the White House. He gave a formal speech during which he said that while he opposed slavery, he also felt that blacks and whites were different and should not try to coexist in the same society. Some historians have pointed to this speech as evidence that Lincoln was a racist. His speech undoubtedly came as an insult to many African Americans. But it also probably worked to calm Northerners who now felt they could rely on Lincoln to support a colonization plan.

A few days later, Horace Greeley, the editor of the *New York Tribune* newspaper, printed an article about Lincoln's actions—or in this case, inaction. In an article titled "The Prayer of Twenty Millions," Greeley skewered Lincoln for not moving swiftly and decisively to abolish slavery.

Lincoln responded to Greeley two days later. He wrote, "If I could save the Union without freeing any slave, I would do it, and if I could save it by freeing all the slaves, I would do it,

Horace Greeley was a staunch abolitionist and the editor of an influential newspaper. He criticized Lincoln's slow progress toward emancipation, but later praised the president's Proclamation.

and if I could save it by freeing some and leaving others alone, I would also do that." What no one knew yet was that Lincoln had already settled on the last option. But still—he was waiting for just the right time. It was less than a month away.

THE RIGHT MOMENT

When Lincoln first read the Proclamation to his cabinet in July 1862, there was one objection. William Seward, the secretary of state, suggested to the president that his timing was off. The Union was losing the war. If Lincoln issued the Proclamation immediately, it might be interpreted as a desperate act from the Union, trying to appear more powerful than it actually was. Lincoln had not considered this possible consequence. He decided Seward had a good point. Rather than release the Proclamation in July, he would wait until the Union was doing better. That way, the Proclamation would be seen as strengthening the Union cause—not trying to save it altogether. Patiently, Lincoln waited, occasionally tinkering with the document's wording. He recalled, "From time to time, I added or changed a line, touching it up here and there, anxiously watching the progress of events."

Thousands died at the bloody Battle of Antietam in the fall of 1862, but the narrow Union victory gave Lincoln the opportunity he wanted to introduce the Emancipation Proclamation.

September 17, 1862, gave Lincoln the event he wanted. The Battle of Antietam (also called the Battle of Sharpsburg), in Maryland, remains the bloodiest day in American history, with more than twenty-two thousand soldiers killed or wounded. By the end of the day, the Union had eked out a victory—of sorts. Union general George McClellan had more troops at his command than the Confederacy's Robert E. Lee, but McClellan failed to take advantage of the situation for a decisive Union win. Rather than being completely overwhelmed, Lee's army was able to retreat and regroup. Thus, neither side really won the battle, but it provided a boost to the Union cause, and Lincoln judged that it was enough for what he wanted. Five days after Antietam, on September 22, Lincoln went public.

Chapter 4

THE HUNDRED DAYS

Affter the Battle of Antietam, Lincoln's goal, still, was to preserve the Union. Abolitionists blasted him for dragging his feet on emancipation, but Lincoln did not want to destroy the South. Thus, on September 22, he issued a preliminary Proclamation. It was his way of giving the South one last chance.

The Proclamation outlined Lincoln's intentions, but it didn't take effect immediately. Instead, it served as an official warning, an ultimatum to the Confederacy: Stop the war, and return to the Union. Lincoln gave the Southern states one hundred days to decide. If they did not end the rebellion, the Proclamation would go into effect on January 1, 1863.

IDEAS IN SQUARE FEET

Lincoln was known for his masterful command of language. He was eloquent in both his speech and his writing. Yet the

FRANCIS BICKNELL CARPENTER

In 1864, the artist Francis Bicknell Carpenter painted a picture to commemorate the day that Lincoln first read the Emancipation Proclamation to his cabinet. Carpenter lived at the White House for six months to meet with the president and work on his enormous painting, which was 9 by 14.5 feet (2.7 by 4.4 meters). The finished painting received mixed reviews from critics, while Lincoln himself said, "It is as good as it can be made." Carpenter later wrote a book about his experiences, *Six Months at the White House with Abraham Lincoln*, which proved far more popular than his painting.

Carpenter tried to get Congress to buy his commemorative painting but was refused. The artist later sold it to a private buyer, who donated it. It now hangs in the U.S. Capitol.

Proclamation lacked any of the president's signature style. It was dry. It was dull. In 1948, historian Richard Hofstadter remarked that the document had the "moral grandeur of a bill of lading." In other words, it was a snore. A couple of weeks after the preliminary Proclamation was issued, the Communist leader Karl Marx praised Lincoln's actions, but noted the document sounded like a report written by one lawyer to another. Marx wrote, "Other people claim to be 'fighting for an idea,' when it is for them a matter of square feet of land. Lincoln, even when he is motivated by an idea, talks about 'square feet.'"

In fact, this was exactly what Lincoln intended. The president was perfectly capable of using soaring, inspiring language that would praise the cause of freedom. However, his goal was not to defend his action by writing about its moral correctness. Instead, he was more concerned about making sure the Proclamation was legal and could stand up in court should anyone try to fight it.

At the time, the nation's Supreme Court was comprised mostly of justices from the South. Just five years earlier, in 1857, it was almost the same group of judges that had decided the famous Dred Scott case. In this ruling, a slave named Dred Scott tried to sue for his freedom on the grounds that he had lived with his master in the free state of Illinois, as well as the free Wisconsin Territory (the present-day state of Minnesota). The Court decided 7–2 against Scott. Chief Justice Roger Taney wrote that because Scott was African American, he could not be considered a citizen of the United States and thus had no legal right to sue.

Lincoln knew the Supreme Court justices were mostly opposed to abolition. If a chink in the legal reasoning could be

When Dred Scott protested his status as a slave, based on the fact that he had lived in a free state, the Supreme Court had to make a decision. It ruled against him, prolonging the institution of slavery.

found, he feared, then the Court would likely rule in favor of slavery. Thus, he worked hard to make sure the Proclamation was bulletproof, legally speaking.

In addition, the Proclamation was actually quite limited in its scope. It would not, in one grand stroke, "free the slaves." Instead, it would apply only to slaves in the rebellious Southern states. The border states that were still loyal to the Union were excluded. So were certain areas that were under Union control, even if they were in the South. In addition, while the Proclamation would declare the slaves free, words were not the same as actions. In reality, the order could not be enforced until the Union Army took possession of an area. Freedom would, by necessity, be a gradual occurrence. Some objected to the severe constraints on the Proclamation. Secretary of State William Seward later said, "We show our sympathy with slavery by emancipating the slaves where we cannot reach them and holding them in bondage where we can set them free." In other words, he doubted the Proclamation's legality in the South and regretted that it did not apply in the slaveholding Union states.

REACTIONS AND EFFECTS

Even as a limited order, and even in its preliminary form, the Proclamation caused an uproar—just as Lincoln had anticipated. During the autumn congressional elections, the Republicans—Lincoln's party—lost ground to pro-slavery Democrats. Before the new Congress could take office, however, the old one tried to strengthen Lincoln's position by reaffirming the Proclamation. It also rejected a proposal

Roger Taney was Chief Justice of the Supreme Court when the Court made its decision in the Dred Scott case in 1857, ruling that because he was African American, Scott could not be considered a citizen.

by Democrats that would make it a "high crime against the Constitution" to interfere with states' rights.

The preliminary Proclamation also took a toll on the Union Army. Enlistment dropped, and desertions increased. Many Northern soldiers had pledged loyalty to the federal cause because they believed they were fighting to preserve the Union. That was, after all, what Lincoln had declared to be the purpose of the war. Now, it seemed, they were fighting for a completely different issue—the emancipation of slaves.

But the idea was catching on, and some soldiers did support emancipation. Levi Hines, a soldier from Vermont, wrote a letter to his parents saying: "The late proclamation of the President makes it a war on Slavery and I am ready to die fighting...for the purpose of ending that hellish curse of our country." In addition, even soldiers who disagreed with the ethics were ready to embrace a policy that would help end the war.

In the South, slave owners were getting anxious. Presidential aide William O. Stoddard wrote after Lincoln issued the preliminary Proclamation, "The President's Emancipation Proclamation is having a greater effect at the South than even its friends anticipated. 'It is the hit bird that flutters.' Every report, from every source, would seem to indicate an immense sensation all over the regions now in rebellion."

No doubt Southern slaveholders realized the Proclamation posed a real threat against their hold on slavery. Not only did they oppose emancipation, but the president's wording had them worried. In the Proclamation, he had ordered that federal forces should not interfere with "any efforts" slaves might use to claim their freedom. Southerners claimed that such wording was practically inviting slaves to rise up against their masters in bloody revolts. Nervous about this possibility, many owners clamped down on their slaves even more. This stance, however, served only to increase racial tensions and give the slaves even more reason to escape if they could.

THE DAY OF JUBILEE

The fall of 1862 progressed, and the hundred days that Lincoln had given the South before its deadline finally passed. During this time, many wondered whether Lincoln would follow through on issuing a final Proclamation. There would be consequences, to be sure, and even those who favored abolition knew it. Even his wife, Mary, was reportedly against it, as she had family members fighting on the Southern side. Would he go through with it? An associate reported in late December, "The President says he would not stop the Proclamation if he could, and could not if he would."

And so, when the New Year arrived, millions awaited his decision. After spending several hours with guests at a White House party, Lincoln finally turned his attention to the matter. But as he lifted his pen to sign the document, his hands trembled. Taking a moment to collect himself, Lincoln realized he was tired, having slept little the night before. In addition, he'd just spent hours shaking hands—it was no wonder that now, it was *his* hands that shook!

Reassured by this logic, Lincoln again took up the pen, and waited a moment to calm the tremors in his hand. He wanted his signature to be clear and strong. If his handwriting was uneven, Lincoln feared that it would be interpreted

Mary Todd Lincoln, the president's wife, was keenly interested in politics and her husband's career. During the Civil War, she often shared her opinions and offered advice to the president.

as evidence that he had doubts. Finally, he signed the document, laid down the pen, and gave a small laugh. Then he looked up at the other men in the room and said, "That will do."

As the news became official, African Americans proclaimed it a "Day of Jubilee," referring to the biblical concept of a time when sins were pardoned and slaves set free. Celebrations began all over the country, from New York City to Washington, from Boston to Philadelphia. Thousands of copies of the Proclamation were printed and distributed to Union military officers and throughout the South. Most slaves could not read, but they could listen—and they did, as word spread about what Lincoln had done. The word was whispered, then shouted, from one mouth to another: "Free!"

Chapter 5

A NEW COURSE

A hundred days passed between when Lincoln issued the preliminary Proclamation and when he signed the final version. Historians have described those months as perhaps the most difficult time of Lincoln's presidency—the worst period in years that were already marked by bloodshed. Lincoln came into office during an immense national crisis and never once got a break from the stress of trying to preside over "a house divided." But he didn't waver. Lincoln recognized that the Proclamation was more than an executive order, more than a measure taken for military necessity. It would forever change America—the only question was how.

THE FINAL WORD

During those tense three months, the president had modified the Proclamation. Some of it involved tinkering with the wording, but other changes were more substantial. For one thing, all mention of the colonization idea was gone. Some historians believe that the suggestion had been included originally as a way to appease people nervous about assimilating the slave population. But, now that Lincoln was acting without the cooperation from the states, he removed it. Also gone was the idea of gradual, compensated emancipation. The South had rejected that offer, and now, Lincoln took it off the table. He had declared freedom with his signature, and it would be enforced as soon as Union soldiers could make it happen.

In previous drafts, Lincoln had declared the slaves free "forever." But in the final version Lincoln chose a more conservative route. He knew that his proclamation could not last "forever." In fact, he was banking on it being legal by specifically making it a wartime measure. Not wanting even the slightest weakness that could be legally challenged, he removed the word.

Another change involved the actions of former slaves after they were freed. The preliminary Proclamation had ordered the federal government and military not to interfere with "any efforts" slaves might make to achieve their freedom. The final version used more careful language. It directed the government to "recognize and maintain" the freedom of former slaves, but it also cautioned those slaves not to engage in violence against whites and to work diligently for fair wages. This modification was intended to appease Southerners who felt that Lincoln's original language could lead to a slave revolt.

Lincoln also went so far as to offer work to freed slaves—in the military itself. It was just one sentence, but this invitation gave the Union a powerful new weapon in the war. Not only were slaves now allowed to leave their masters, taking away their help to the South, but they could actually contribute to the Union side. They could have a role in their own freedom. For many African Americans, it was an irresistible offer, and they took up the call.

Frederick Douglass was among those who signed this poster from the 1860s. It recruited African Americans to fight for the Union in the Civil War, implying that their freedom hung in the balance.

SLAVES TO SOLDIERS

Most white people, even those who opposed slavery, did not believe blacks should serve in the army. White people con-sidered blacks to be mentally inferior and unfit to act as soldiers. Nevertheless, in the summer of 1862, Congress passed a law allowing blacks to enlist in the Union Army. Lincoln decided that these new enlistees could serve as general workers, but not sol-diers. However, the president's attitude eventually changed— and so did the opinion of many Union soldiers. Charles Wills, from Illinois, wrote, "I never thought I would, but I am getting strongly in favor of arming [African Americans], and am becoming so blind that I can't see why they will not make good soldiers."

As a result of the Proclamation, in May 1863 the government established the Bureau of Colored Troops. This department was in charge of recruiting and training the African Americans who wished

"MAKE WAY FOR LIBERTY!"

A drawing of a black soldier dressed in a Union blue uniform depicts how African Americans fought alongside white soldiers in their joint cause to "Make Way for Liberty."

to serve in the war. Over the next few years, some 180,000 African Americans joined the federal cause. About 60 percent of those came from the Confederacy, and another 25 percent from the border states.

While the United States Colored Troops (USCT) was a step in the right direction, racism still factored into the administration of the newly formed black regiments. For example, only whites were permitted to serve as officers. That created a problem in finding men who were both capable of leading and had an open-minded attitude toward black soldiers. Except in special circumstances, blacks were also barred from performing other specialized jobs in the military, such as being doctors or chaplains.

And then there was money. Black soldiers earned only about half of what white troops received. White soldiers were paid $13 a month. Blacks made only $10, and $3 of that was required to pay for clothing, which was issued free to white soldiers. Fortunately, in June 1864, Congress passed legislation that said all Union soldiers—black and white—would receive the same pay and the same supplies.

The African Americans who decided to join the military also encountered risks beyond the normal ones. Soldiers at war must always face violence and possible death, but blacks faced even graver risks. Those who were captured by Confederates were harshly treated or even killed. Some of them were sold back into slavery.

However, as Lincoln had hoped, as African Americans swelled the ranks of the Union side, they helped swing the momentum of the war in the Union's favor. Black troops played a key role in the seven-week Siege of Vicksburg

SIEGE OF VICKSBURG.

Union soldiers man their stations under the command of General Ulysses Grant during the Siege of Vicksburg, a grueling standoff that lasted weeks before Confederate forces surrendered.

(Mississippi) in 1863, where Union general Ulysses S. Grant defeated Confederate forces. The federal victory at Vicksburg is often considered a key turning point of the war.

SHIFTING PRIORITIES

At the onset of the war, Lincoln had stated that his goal was to preserve the Union. That was the point of the war, not to pass judgment on slavery and try to abolish it. But the Proclamation changed that. When Lincoln signed that document, the character of the war changed. It was about slavery now. The president had given up his earlier pledge not to interfere with slavery in the South because he saw no other way to bring the conflict to an end.

Lincoln wrote, "The proclamation was issued for two reasons. The first and chief reason was this, I felt a great impulse

SOLD FOR SOLDIERS

The original manuscript of the Emancipation Proclamation did not go into some vault in the White House. Instead, later in 1863, Lincoln donated it to a charity that helped wounded soldiers. It sold in an auction for $3,000 (about $55,000 today). The document later ended up with the Chicago Historical Society, but it was destroyed in 1871, during the Great Chicago Fire. However, additional copies of the Proclamation had been printed and signed by Lincoln. They were also sold to raise money for soldiers. Some of those copies still exist.

moving me to do justice to five or six millions of people. The second reason was that I believed it would be a club in our hands with which we could whack the rebels. In other words, it would shorten the war. I believed that under the Constitution I had a right to issue the proclamation as a 'military necessity.'"

Even so, Lincoln took an enormous risk issuing the final document. He was attempting to end slavery, and connected to that action was the idea that blacks would have rights. Would the people accept such a change? Not all would, of course. But Lincoln had—and others would, too. Silas Shearer, an Iowa soldier, wrote to his wife in September 1863, "My eyes don't see as they did when I left home." Previously, he had opposed abolition, but now he had changed his mind. "I say Amen to it and I believe the Best thing that has been done Since the War broke out is the Emancipation Proclimation [sic]."

THE FIGHT CONTINUES

Nonetheless, the Proclamation hardened the resistance of the South. With it, Lincoln had withdrawn his attempts at compromise and reconciliation. No longer did Southerners even have the option to gradually end slavery and be compensated for their property. Now they had no incentive to stop the fighting. Their only chance to preserve slavery was to continue the war. By now, however, the South was starting to move to a more defensive position. Whether it was legal or not, their slaves were leaving. The Proclamation did not instantly free the slaves, but it set the country on a path from which there was no going back.

"Take the baby; what in hell do we want of the baby?"

Entitled "The Maddest Man in all Maryland," this illustration (circa 1865) shows a farmer being caught in the act of trying to return freed slaves to the South.

Lincoln hoped the Proclamation would shorten the war—and perhaps it did. Nonetheless, there were still two and a half long years to go before the Confederacy would finally fall and the country would technically be reunited. But it would be a battered nation when it did, half of it beaten and bitter, all of it exhausted. Lincoln himself would not live to see the day the war ended, much less how his country would fare afterward. But he knew that his wartime measures would not last. In 1858, Lincoln had predicted that eventually, the United States would have to decide one way or the other: slavery, or not? "A house divided," he had said, would not stand. He had laid the foundation to run the "house" one way. Now it would be another kind of fight to keep it standing.

Chapter 6

BEARING FRUIT

"He was so *slow*." That was the main complaint abolitionists had with Lincoln's progress toward issuing the Emancipation Proclamation. But Lincoln was cautious. He did not intend to do anything that he would have to reverse later. As such, he would not be hurried—no matter how his critics might object. He wrote, "A man watches his pear-tree day after day, impatient for the ripening of the fruit. Let him attempt to *force* the process, and he may spoil both fruit and tree. But let him patiently *wait*, and the ripe pear at length falls into his lap!"

INSTITUTION VS. CONSTITUTION

If emancipation was the first pear, now Lincoln set his sights on a more bountiful harvest. The South's "peculiar institution" of slavery was constitutional and did not violate the underlying law of the country. It was that roadblock that had given Lincoln so much trouble. It had guided all his actions—how he wrote the Proclamation, the regions where it applied, and when he issued it. Having crafted it as a wartime measure, Lincoln knew that when the war ended, so would the Proclamation. Its expiration date got closer as the Union began to take control. But Lincoln also felt there was no turning back, morally.

Hundreds of thousands of slaves were finally getting a taste of freedom, and many of them were actively fighting for it. How could it be snatched away once again?

Lincoln began to work on finding a permanent solution. Ultimately, that meant changing, or amending, the Constitution. The Founding Fathers had purposely made this difficult. The Constitution guaranteed and protected certain rights. They did not want it to be too easy for lawmakers to take them away. However, they had also recognized that times change, circumstances change, and people's opinions change. It should not be impossible to adapt the Constitution if it were truly necessary. With slavery, Lincoln believed it was.

THE THIRTEENTH AMENDMENT

On New Year's Day 1864, exactly one year after the Emancipation Proclamation had gone into effect, Illinois congressman Isaac Arnold visited Lincoln. He told the president he wished for three things in the coming year: the end of the war; an amendment to abolish slavery; and the president's reelection. Upon hearing these wishes, Lincoln responded: "I think my friend, I would be willing to accept the first two by way of compromise." In other words, Lincoln was saying he would give up his desire for reelection if it meant the nation could go forward in the way he felt was best. As it happened, however, Arnold got the third thing, but not the first two.

There was progress, though. In the spring of 1864, Congress considered an amendment that would abolish slavery. The Senate passed the amendment, but it failed in the House of Representatives. Nonetheless, Lincoln was laying the groundwork. When the amendment once again came before

Throngs of people celebrated in the nation's House of Representatives on January 31, 1865, the day that Congress passed the thirteenth constitutional amendment, which abolished slavery.

SLAVERY FOR EVER.

Congress, Lincoln took a hands-on approach. He made political promises and granted favors in return for votes. For some Democratic congressmen who opposed the amendment, Lincoln even agreed to release their relatives from military prisons. The ethics of Lincoln's actions can be debated, but they were certainly within his presidential power, and by late 1864, he was willing to use whatever leverage he had. His efforts paid off. The House passed the amendment in January 1865; the required number of states ratified it; and it went into effect in December 1865.

Lincoln lived to see the amendment pass, but not its effect. Nor did he survive to see the goal for which he had worked tirelessly his entire presidency: peace. He was assassinated in April 1865. Less than a week before Lincoln's death, Confederate general Robert E. Lee surrendered to Ulysses S. Grant at the Battle of Appomattox, marking the beginning of the end of the war, but it would be several more months before all fighting ceased and the remaining Confederate forces surrendered.

RECONSTRUCTION

By now, the country was on the long and wearisome path called Reconstruction. For that is what it was: the country was in a shambles. Both sides faced huge financial burdens. The economy was a wreck. Farms, railroads, ports, and entire cities had been destroyed as the war raged. Not only did the country need to be physically reconstructed, it had to be mentally rebuilt as well. The psychological damage struck at the heart of almost every American. Hundreds of thousands of men had been killed or wounded—hardly a family was left untouched. Racial tensions were no better, and perhaps even worse. No piece of paper, not even a constitutional amendment, could erase decades of prejudice.

Throughout the South, governments elected the same officials who had supported slavery. To thwart the rights of African Americans, they began to institute the "Black Codes." These laws severely limited the rights and opportunities of blacks. Many blacks found that although they were technically free, they were unable to fully participate in society. They could not vote. They were hard-pressed to find jobs.

FORTY ACRES AND A MULE

As Union armies marched through the South, thousands of African American slaves were freed—but a problem remained. They had their freedom, but little else. They had depended on their masters for work. To help solve this problem, Union general William Tecumseh Sherman issued an order granting the newly freed slaves forty acres of land to farm for themselves. Mules weren't included in the order, but the army did have extra mules, which it donated for the freedmen to use. Sherman's plan was only temporary, however, and during Reconstruction many former slaves ended up working for whites under the sharecropping system.

They were excluded from many public places. Many slaves, left with no other option, returned to their former masters and engaged in sharecropping. In this system, they worked the land as they always had, in return for a small share of the crop. Unfortunately, it was difficult to make a living under this system. Financially, many were no better off than they had been as slaves.

Neither Lincoln nor his successor, Andrew Johnson, took a punitive attitude toward the South. They favored a more moderate approach. Radical Republicans in Congress, however, had different ideas. By 1866, they had gained enough power that they could block attempts to put former Southern leaders back into control and force the South to give blacks more rights. The intent of the Radical Republicans might have been worthy, but the lack of unity in the government further slowed the progress of Reconstruction. By the late 1870s, Southern whites had regained enough power that they were able to oppress blacks more. Most historians consider Reconstruction a failure in terms of furthering African American rights.

It was a bleak picture, but there was some progress. Two more constitutional amendments were passed in the years after the Civil War. In 1868, the Fourteenth Amendment gave citizenship to all people born in the United States, which meant that slaves were now legally able to seek justice under the law. The Fifteenth Amendment, passed in 1870, gave all male citizens—now including blacks—the right to vote. However, Southern cities and states often got around this law by requiring blacks to take a literacy test or pay a tax before they were allowed to vote. Unfortunately, most blacks could not pass the test or afford the tax.

LINCOLN'S LEGACY

Throughout the remainder of the nineteenth century and the first half of the twentieth, living conditions for most African Americans continued to be inferior to that of whites. Certain laws in the South prevented blacks from operating on an equal footing with whites. They were forbidden to go into certain hotels and restaurants; they were turned away at the polls; they were denied jobs and housing based on their race. In some cases they were the targets of violence, all because of the color of their skin. Some called Lincoln the Great Emancipator, but as time passed, some of the shine of this accomplishment rubbed off.

In the 1950s and 1960s, the civil rights movement began taking off. African Americans noted that a hundred years after the Emancipation Proclamation, blacks still weren't really free. They weren't physically enslaved, but they weren't treated the same as whites, nor did they have the same social and economic opportunities. Finishing what Lincoln had started—gaining true emancipation—became the goal.

Had Lincoln really made a difference? Later historians criticized him. They questioned whether the Emancipation Proclamation had ever been legal and the extent of its benefit, since it freed only some slaves. But as more scholars piece together what is known about Lincoln and the character of the country at the time in the 1860s, it appears the president knew what he was doing. Yes, he was slow, but he was also deliberate, wanting his actions to stick. He cared more about the ultimate effect of his decisions than he did of what people thought of him at the time.

Police protected African American citizens at a Memphis school after it was desegregated in 1957. Almost one hundred years after the Civil War, the fight for civil rights continued in America, especially in the South.

The words of the Emancipation Proclamation were often ignored, but they were *there*. For better or worse, they would change America. They would be the reason that people remembered the sixteenth president, and Lincoln knew it. "I never, in my life, felt more certain that I was doing right, than I do in signing this paper," he said. "If my name ever goes into history it will be for this act, and my whole soul is in it."

TIMELINE

1850 The Fugitive Slave Act is passed.

1854 The Republican Party is formed.

1857 In the case of *Dred Scott v. Sandford*, the Supreme Court rules that slaves are not citizens and do not have the legal rights to sue for freedom.

1858 Abraham Lincoln runs for the U.S. Senate but loses the seat to Stephen Douglas.

February 27, 1860 Lincoln gives a speech opposing the expansion of slavery into the federal territories.

November 6, 1860 Lincoln is elected president.

December 20, 1860 South Carolina becomes the first state to secede from the Union.

April 12, 1861 Shots are fired at Fort Sumter, officially beginning the Civil War.

May 24, 1861 Union general Benjamin Butler harbors fugitive slaves, saying they are enemy property.

August 30, 1861 Union general John Frémont declares martial law in Missouri and declares slaves owned by slave owners in rebellion against the Union to be free.

Fall 1861 Lincoln begins attempts to convince the border states to accept a plan of voluntary, gradual, and compensated emancipation but is unsuccessful.

Spring 1862 Lincoln begins writing the Emancipation Proclamation.

July 22, 1862 Lincoln first introduces a draft of the Emancipation Proclamation to his cabinet.

September 17, 1862 The Battle of Antietam gives the Union a qualified victory.

September 22, 1862 Lincoln issues the preliminary Emancipation Proclamation.

January 1, 1863 Lincoln signs the final Emancipation Proclamation.

January 31, 1865 The Thirteenth Amendment to the Constitution, abolishing slavery, receives final approval from Congress.

April 15, 1865 Lincoln is assassinated.

1866 President Andrew Johnson declares an official end to the Civil War; Reconstruction begins.

1868 Congress passes the Fourteenth Amendment, establishing blacks as citizens.

1870 Congress passes the Fifteenth Amendment, giving all male citizens—including blacks—the right to vote.

GLOSSARY

ABOLISH To put an end to something.

AMEND To change.

CABINET The group of senior advisers to the president.

CHAPLAIN A religious leader.

COMPENSATE To give money or some other valuable in an exchange.

CONFEDERACY The Southern side during the U.S. Civil War.

CONFISCATE To take something away, often for a political or legal reason.

DELEGATES Representatives.

ELOQUENT Having the ability to use language persuasively and well.

EMANCIPATION The act of freeing or liberating someone from another's control.

FUGITIVE Someone who is actively hiding from or evading law enforcement officials.

INFRINGE To wrongfully limit or intrude upon another.

JURISDICTION The area where a government or other body has authority.

MARTIAL LAW Civil rule by the military, usually imposed temporarily, under extreme circumstances.

MUTINY An uprising, often violent, against another authority or power.

RADICAL Extreme, outside the norm.

RATIFY To accept and approve.

RESCIND To take back or undo.

SECEDE To formally break away.

ULTIMATUM A final offer demanding a decision.

UNION The Northern side during the Civil War.

Abraham Lincoln Institute
94 Cumberland Court
Frederick, MD 21702
E-mail: cevans885@gmail.com
Website: http://www.lincoln-institute.org
The Abraham Lincoln Institute fosters scholarly research
    into Lincoln's life and career, and provides educational
    resources and opportunities.

Abraham Lincoln Presidential Library and Museum
212 N. 6th Street
Springfield, IL 62701
(217) 558-8844
Website: http://www.illinois.gov/alplm
The Lincoln library and museum house documents and
    records from Lincoln's personal life and his presidency
    and have exhibits detailing the president's legacy.

Leadership Conference on Civil and Human Rights
1629 K Street NW, 10th Floor
Washington, DC 20006
(202) 466- 3311
Website: http://www.civilrights.org
The Leadership Conference was founded in 1950 by leaders
    from several civil rights groups, focusing on passing leg-
    islation to ensure civil rights. The conference continues
    such work today.

National Association for the Advancement of Colored People
    (NAACP)
4805 Mt. Hope Drive

Baltimore, MD 21215

(410) 580-5777

Website: http://www.naacp.org

For more than a century, the NAACP has worked to gain equality for African Americans and other minorities in civil rights, economic justice, and other areas.

National Civil War Museum

One Lincoln Circle at Reservoir Park

Harrisburg, PA 17103

(717) 260-1861

Website: http://www.nationalcivilwarmuseum.org

The Civil War Museum has an extensive collection of artifacts, photographs, and documents that illustrate and help interpret the events and issues of the Civil War.

WEBSITES

Due to the changing nature of Internet links, Rosen Publishing has developed an online list of websites related to the subject of this book. This site is updated regularly. Please use this link to access the list:

http://www.rosenlinks.com/CCRM/Emanc

FOR FURTHER READING

Bolden, Tonya. *Emancipation Proclamation: Lincoln and the Dawn of Liberty.* New York, NY: Abrams Books for Young Readers, 2013.

Capek, Michael. *Civil Rights Movement.* Minneapolis, MN: ABDO Publishing, 2013.

Carlisle, Rodney P., ed. *The Civil War and Reconstruction: 1860 to 1876.* New York, NY: Facts on File, 2009.

Ford, Carin T. *The Emancipation Proclamation, Lincoln, and Slavery Through Primary Sources.* Berkeley Heights, NJ: Enslow, 2013.

Freedman, Russell. *Abraham Lincoln and Frederick Douglass: The Story Behind an American Friendship.* New York, NY: Clarion Books, 2012.

Freedman, Russell. *Lincoln: A Photobiography.* New York, NY: HMH Books for Young Readers, 1989.

Holzer, Harold. *Lincoln: How Abraham Lincoln Ended Slavery in America: A Companion Book for Young Readers to the Steven Spielberg Film.* New York, NY: Newmarket for It Books, 2012.

Knudsen, Shannon. *When Were the First Slaves Set Free During the Civil War?: And Other Questions About the Emancipation Proclamation.* Minneapolis, MN: Lerner Publishing Group, 2010.

Krensky, Stephen. *The Emancipation Proclamation.* Tarrytown, NY: Marshall Cavendish Children's Books, 2011.

Marcovitz, Hal. *The Constitution and the Founding of a New Nation.* San Diego, CA: ReferencePoint Press, 2013.

Murphy, Jim. *A Savage Thunder: Antietam and the Bloody Road to Freedom.* New York, NY: Margaret K. McElderry Books, 2009.

O'Reilly, Bill, and Dwight Jon Zimmerman. *Lincoln's Last Days: The Shocking Assassination That Changed America*

Forever. New York, NY: Henry Holt Books for Young Readers, 2012.

Prentzas, G. S. *The Emancipation Proclamation.* New York, NY: Children's Press, 2011.

Stanchak, John. *Eyewitness Civil War.* New York, NY: DK Publishing, 2011.

Sterngass, Jon. *Frederick Douglass.* New York, NY: Chelsea House, 2009.

Stone, Tanya Lee. *DK Biography: Abraham Lincoln.* New York, NY: DK Children, 2005.

Trotman, C. James. *Frederick Douglass: A Biography.* Westport, CT: Greenwood, 2011.

Woog, Adam. *The Emancipation Proclamation: Ending Slavery in America.* New York, NY: Chelsea House, 2009.

BIBLIOGRAPHY

Associated Press. "Letters Suggest Lincoln Wanted to Buy
    Slaves for $400 Apiece in 'Gradual Emancipation.'"
    FoxNews.com, March 5, 2008. Retrieved August 5, 2013
    (http://www.foxnews.com/story/2008/03/05/letters
    -suggest-lincoln-wanted-to-buy-slaves-for-400-apiece-in
    -gradual).

Blair, William A., and Karen Fisher Younger. *Lincoln's
    Proclamation: Emancipation Reconsidered.* Chapel Hill, NC:
    The University of North Carolina Press, 2009.

Carnahan, Burrus M. *Act of Justice: Lincoln's Emancipation
    Proclamation and the Law of War.* Lexington, KY: The
    University Press of Kentucky, 2007.

Civil War Trust. "10 Facts About the Emancipation
    Proclamation." Retrieved July 11, 2013 (http://www
    .civilwar.org/education/history/emancipation-150
    /10-facts.html).

Gienapp, William E. "Abraham Lincoln and the Border
    States." *Journal of the Abraham Lincoln Association,* 1992.
    Retrieved August 5, 2013 (http://quod.lib.umich.edu
    /j/jala/2629860.0013.104/–abraham-lincoln-and-the
    -border-states?rgn=main;view=fulltext).

Goodheart, Adam. "How Slavery Really Ended in America."
    New York Times Magazine, April 1, 2011. Retrieved July 28,
    2013 (http://www.nytimes.com/2011/04/03/magazine/
    mag-03CivilWar-t.html?pagewanted=all&_r=1&).

Guelzo, Allen. *Lincoln's Emancipation Proclamation: The End of
    Slavery in America.* New York, NY: Simon & Schuster, 2004.

Hallowed Ground Magazine. "'Thenceforward and Forever
    Free': The Emancipation Proclamation and Its Effect on
    the War." Civil War Trust, Fall 2012. Retrieved July 11,

2013 (http://www.civilwar.org/education/history/emancipation-150/thenceforward-and-forever.html).

Holzer, Harold. *Emancipating Lincoln: The Proclamation in Text, Context, and Memory.* Cambridge, MA: Harvard University Press, 2012.

Holzer, Harold, Edna Greene Medford, and Frank J. Williams. *The Emancipation Proclamation: Three Views.* Baton Rouge, LA: Louisiana State University Press, 2006.

Lincoln Institute. "Civil War." Retrieved July 28, 2013 (http://www.mrlincolnandfreedom.org/inside.asp?ID=27).

Lincoln Institute. "Mr. Lincoln's Office: Passage of Thirteenth Amendment." Retrieved July 28, 2013 (http://www.mrlincolnswhitehouse.org/inside.asp?ID=625&subjectID=3).

Mackaman, Tom. "150 Years Since the Emancipation Proclamation." World Socialist Web Site, January 3, 2013. Retrieved July 11, 2013 (http://www.wsws.org/en/articles/2013/01/03/proc-j03.html).

Masur, Louis P. "Liberty Is a Slow Fruit." *American Scholar,* Autumn 2012. Retrieved July 11, 2013 (http://theamericanscholar.org/liberty-is-a-slow-fruit/#.Ul8h5dco7IV).

Masur, Louis P. *Lincoln's Hundred Days: The Emancipation Proclamation and the War for the Union.* Cambridge, MA: The Belknap Press of Harvard University Press, 2012.

McPherson, James M. *Abraham Lincoln and the Second American Revolution.* New York, NY: Oxford University Press, 1991.

National Park Service. "The Civil War's Black Soldiers."
    Retrieved July 28, 2013 (http://www.nps.gov/history
    /history/online_books/civil_war_series/2/sec11.htm).
Owens, Mackubin Thomas. "Lincoln Won the War, But Did
    He Free the Slaves?" The Claremont Institute. Retrieved
    August 5, 2013 (http://www.claremont.org/publications
    /pubid.333/pub_detail.asp).
Vorenberg, Michael. *The Emancipation Proclamation: A
    Brief History with Documents.* Boston, MA: Bedford/St.
    Martin's, 2010.

INDEX

ABOUT THE AUTHOR

Diane Bailey has written about forty nonfiction books for children and teens on topics including sports, celebrities, government, finance, and technology. She has also written several manuscripts of novels for children, and her first adult novel, the murder mystery *Murder A Cappella*, was published in 2012. Bailey also works as an editor for other children's authors. She has two sons and two dogs and lives in Kansas.

PHOTO CREDITS

Cover (Lincoln) © iStockphoto.com/wynnter; cover (background) Three Lions/Hulton Archive/Getty Images; pp. 4, 48 Buyenlarge/Archive Photos/Getty Images; pp. 9, 35 Hulton Archive/Getty Images; pp. 11, 23, 36–37, 53, 54–55 Library of Congress Prints and Photographs Division; p. 13 Culture Club/Hulton Archive/Getty Images; pp. 14–15 Stock Montage/Archive Photos/Getty Images; pp. 20–21, 29, 62–63 MPI/Archive Photos/Getty Images; p. 26 Hulton Archive/Archive Photos/Getty Images; p. 33 FPG/The Image Bank/Getty Images; pp. 40–41 SuperStock/GettyImages; pp. 43, 52, 58 Kean Collection/Archive Photos/Getty Images; p. 45 Encyclopaedia Britannica/Universal Images Group/Getty Images; p. 67 Don Cravens/Time & Life Pictures/Getty Images; cover and interior background images © iStockphoto.com/Victor Pelaez (U. S. Constitution facsimile), © iStockphoto.com/klikk (American flag).

Designer: Nicole Russo; Executive Editor: Hope Lourie Killcoyne; Photo Researcher: Marty Levick